Published in the USA in 2023 by Welbeck Children's Limited
part of the Welbeck Publishing Group
Based in London and Sydney
www.welbeckpublishing.com
Text © 2023 Simon Mugford
Design & Illustration © 2023 Dan Green
ISBN: 978-1-78312-577-7

Writer: Simon Mugford
Designer and Illustrator: Dan Green
Design Manager: Sam James
Senior Commissioning Editor: Suhel Ahmed
Production: Arlene Alexander

Printed in the UK
10 9 8 7 6 5 4 3 2 1

Statistics and records correct as of July 2023

SOCCER SUPERSTARS

MESSI

RULES

SIMON MUGFORD   DAN GREEN

CONTENTS

CHAPTER 1

MESSI IS AWESOME

MESSI!

MESSI!

Is **Lionel Messi** the best soccer player in the world? You are reading this book because you think he is **AWESOME, AMAZING,** and the

GREATEST

player on the **planet,** right?

6

Messi is probably **THE** best player in the world, maybe even...

THE GREATEST PLAYER EVER.

GRRR!

Just don't tell *Cristiano Ronaldo* we said that!

MESS!

SO WHAT MAKES MESSI SO FANTASTIC?

Movement
Small and quick—gets away from defenders.

Dribbling
No player keeps the ball at their feet better than Messi.

Passing
Always delivers the perfect ball to his teammates.

Vision
He creates space and sees chances everywhere.

GOALS!
Of course, **Messi scores goals. LOTS** and **LOTS** and **LOTS** of **GOALS!**

Messi is simply
INCREDIBLE!
10
WOMP!
HE IS THE ULTIMATE
PLAYMAKER!

HOW AMAZING IS *MESSI?*

JUST LOOK AT THE **NUMBERS** . . .

7 . . . times winner of the **BALLON D'OR**

OVER **815** . . . career **GOALS**

10 . . . **LA LIGA** titles

103 ... goals scored for **ARGENTINA**

483 MILLION ... followers on **INSTAGRAM**

474 ... goals scored in **LA LIGA**

MORE THAN $1 BILLION CAREER EARNINGS

MESSI I.D.

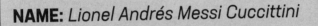

NAME: *Lionel Andrés Messi Cuccittini*

NICKNAME: *The Flea*

DATE OF BIRTH: *June 24, 1987*

PLACE OF BIRTH: *Rosario, Argentina*

HEIGHT: *5 ft 7 in (1.70m)*

POSITION: *Forward*

CLUBS: *Newell's Old Boys (youth team), Barcelona, Paris Saint-Germain*

NATIONAL TEAM: *Argentina*

LEFT OR RIGHT-FOOTED: *Left*

CHAPTER 2

LITTLE LEO

13

Lionel Messi was born in a town called Rosario in **Argentina** in **1987.** Everyone in his family loved playing and watching soccer, so Messi did, too!

Just as soon as he could walk, Messi started playing soccer in the park with his brothers and cousins. They were all **older,** and much **BIGGER** than he was, but Lionel soon became the best player on the field.

They called him **"Titch"** because he was so small, but Messi didn't mind. It made him want to **play harder** and **become even better.**

When he was just **five** Leo joined his first club, **Grandoli.** His brothers Rodrigo and Matias played there, and his **grandmother** Celia took him to training.

Messi was already fantastic at **passing, dribbling,** and **scoring** goals and the coach at Grandoli was amazed.

WOW, THIS BOY IS INCREDIBLE!

Leo trained really hard and his grandmother

was always there, **cheering him on.**

Leo was the smallest kid at school but he was the **best soccer player** by far. When they played soccer at recess, **nobody could get near him!**

Soon, the **whole town** of Rosario had heard about the **amazing little kid** who played for Grandoli. Lots of people came to watch Messi's amazing skills.

It was **Messi's dream** to play for his local team,

NEWELL'S OLD BOYS.

His dream came true when he was just **six**.

20

At first, Messi played a **seven-a-side** game called **Baby Soccer.**

In his first game for Newell's, he scored **four goals** in a 6-0 win.

Messi's team were so good, nobody beat them for **three** years. They were known as

THE MACHINE OF '87

because that was the year most of the players were born.

Why is Messi like a baby?

Because he's good at dribbling!

One time, Messi was **missing** for the start of a game. When he finally turned up at halftime, the team were losing 1-0. Leo had been **stuck in the toilet!**

Messi came on, **scored three goals,** and Newell's won **3–1!**

CHAPTER 3

MESSI MAGIC

Messi started playing **proper soccer** when he was **eleven.** Messi and his team were so good, they beat opponents by as many as 15 goals! Some teams would stop the game after **Newell's** scored six.

The **Machine of '87** won

everything—they were

UNSTOPPABLE!

In six years at Newell's, the young Messi

scored more than

500 GOALS.

Newell's Old Boys knew that Leo was very special. People said he was going to be a **legend,** like the famous Argentinian player **MARADONA.**

When the first team played, Messi would entertain the crowd at halftime or before the game by playing **"keepy-uppies."**

ONE TIME HE DID 1,200!

Leo was very close to his grandmother. She had taken him to practice at **Grandoli** and his first days at **Newell's.** She died when he was 10 and Leo missed her very much.

Leo celebrated his first goal after she died by pointing both fingers to the sky.

IT WAS TO REMEMBER HIS GRANDMA.

"I HAVE SEEN THE PLAYER WHO WILL INHERIT MY PLACE IN ARGENTINE FOOTBALL AND HIS NAME IS MESSI."

Diego Maradona

CHAPTER 4

BARCELONA BOUND

When Messi was **10,** he started taking **medicine** to help him grow **taller,** but the medicine was very **expensive.** If he was going to be a top player, Leo and his family had to find a club that would pay for it.

ARGENTINA

That club was thousands of miles away in **Spain.**

Leo signed for **Barcelona** when he was just **13.** The club had never signed such a **young** player from so far away before. And he was so **small!**

Messi's first **contract** was written out on a **napkin** in a restaurant!

Soon, it was obvious that Messi was a **very, very special soccer player.**

I always use a napkin when I'm eating!

Why?

Because I'm a **Messi** eater!

35

Although, Leo's dad came to live with him in **Barcelona,** Leo missed his **friends** and the rest of his **family.**

GERARD PIQUE

CESC FABREGAS

Then Messi made two new friends, defender **Gerard Pique** and midfielder **Cesc Fabregas.** Leo was **much, much happier.**

They gave Leo his nickname:

THE FLEA.

Why do they call him **"The Flea"?**

Because he is **small, fast,** and a constant menace!

SCRATCH! SCRATCH!

After training, the three boys would spend hours playing FIFA on the **PlayStation** together.

Leo was the best, of course!

Messi, Pique, and **Fabregas** were

part of the

GENERATION OF '87,

OR THE

BABY DREAM TEAM.

In the **2002–2003** season, in the under-16s, they won the league and the Spanish and Catalan Cups. They were **unbeaten** all season and Messi scored **36 goals** in **30 games.**

INCREDIBLE!

ER, I CAN'T SEE PROPERLY!

Leo began the 2003 Catalan Cup final **wearing a face mask** because of an injury. But he couldn't play in it, so he took it off. Then he **scored twice** in **10 minutes!**

That game became known as

THE GAME OF THE MASK.

CHAPTER 5

GOLDEN GOALS

GOAL #1

Messi picked up the ball **in his own half**

and then went past two players.

Running at speed with the ball glued to his feet, Messi **zipped and turned** his way through **three** more opponents . . .

. . . before **dribbling** past the goalie and scoring.

AN AMAZING **SOLO** GOAL!

Barcelona's fans voted this the *best-ever Barcelona goal.*

GOAL #2

MAY 30, 2015

COPA DEL REY FINAL

Athletic Bilbao 1-3 Barcelona

Another **superb solo** effort from Messi. He took the ball on the right, near the touchline.

He zipped past **one** . . .

two . . .

three . . .

players and was in the box.

He passed one more player and took a shot–

GOALLLLL!

What's the **second-best** Barcelona goal?

This one.

GOAL #3

APRIL 27, 2011

CHAMPIONS LEAGUE SEMIFINAL, FIRST LEG

Real Madrid 0-2 Barcelona

BOFFFF!

Playing against Barcelona's great rivals **Real Madrid** in a massive Champions League game, Messi again made a solo run, **straight down the middle** with the ball.

He got past a Madrid defense that included **Sergio Ramos** to score his **second goal of the match.**

GENIUS!

Yep, this is the fans' *third-best* Barcelona goal!

"IS MESSI A REAL PLAYER OR A PLAYSTATION CHARACTER?"

Colombia striker Radamel Falcao

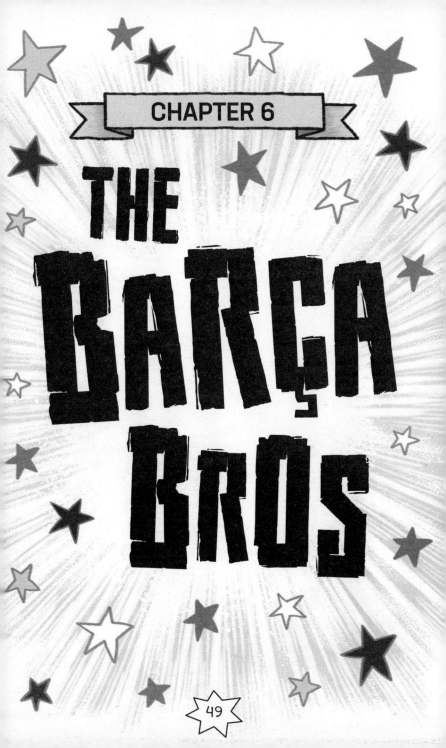

CHAPTER 6

THE BARÇA BROS

49

Messi played in **La Liga** for the first time in **2004.** Barcelona's superstar striker at the time was the Brazilian, **Ronaldinho.** He called Leo his **"little brother"** and they became good friends.

Ronaldinho set up Messi's first Barcelona goal against Albacete in 2005. From then on, the two of them, along with **Samuel Eto'o,** made a **great attacking trio.**

MANY *INCREDIBLE* STRIKERS HAVE PLAYED FOR *BARCELONA.*

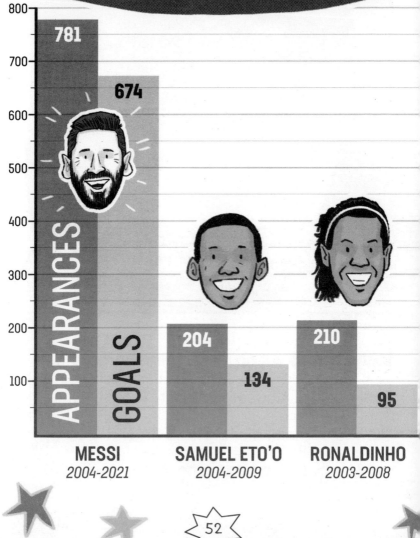

APPEARANCES / **GOALS**

	Appearances	Goals
MESSI 2004-2021	781	674
SAMUEL ETO'O 2004-2009	204	134
RONALDINHO 2003-2008	210	95

From **2004 to 2015,** Messi played with the Spanish star midfielders **Xavi Hernandez** and **Andres Iniesta**.

Manager **Pep Guardiola** taught his players to move and pass quickly, and always keep possession.

The Spanish called it **Tiki-taka.**

IT WORKED!

With **Xavi** and **Iniesta, Messi** won **La Liga** seven times, the **Copa del Rey** three times, and the **Champions League** four times.

In the three seasons from **2014** to **2017**, Barcelona had the amazing attacking trio of **Messi, Luis Suarez,** and **Neymar.** They were known as

Together, **MSN** were **UNSTOPPABLE.**

In their first season playing together, Barcelona won the **TRIPLE** of **La Liga, the Copa del Rey,** and **the Champions League.**

IN TOTAL, THEY SCORED **364** GOALS AND RECORDED **211** ASSISTS.

"IT WAS AN HONOR TO BE THE COACH OF THE BEST PLAYER I HAVE EVER SEEN AND PROBABLY THE BEST I WILL SEE."

Pep Guardiola

CHAPTER 7

CHAMPIONS LEAGUE CHAMP

Messi's record in the **Champions League** is just incredible. Barcelona have won the title **FOUR** times with Messi.

MAY 17, 2006

STADE DE FRANCE, SAINT-DENIS, FRANCE

Barcelona 2-1 Arsenal

Messi didn't actually play in the final.

MAY 27, 2009

STADIO OLIMPICO, ROME

Barcelona 2-0 Manchester United

MAY 28, 2011

WEMBLEY STADIUM, LONDON

Barcelona 3-1 Manchester United

JUNE 6, 2015

OLIMPIASTADION, BERLIN

Juventus 1-3 Barcelona

CHAMPIONS LEAGUE STAR

TOP CHAMPIONS LEAGUE SCORER

2008-09
9 GOALS

2009-10
8 GOALS

2010-11
12 GOALS

2011-12
14 GOALS

2014-15
10 GOALS

2018-19
12 GOALS

FASTEST PLAYER TO 100 CHAMPIONS LEAGUE GOALS
123 GAMES

MOST CHAMPIONS LEAGUE GROUP STAGE GOALS
78 GOALS

YOUNGEST PLAYER TO SCORE **50 GOALS** IN THE CHAMPIONS LEAGUE

FIRST PLAYER TO SCORE **5 GOALS** IN A CHAMPIONS LEAGUE MATCH

MOST CHAMPIONS LEAGUE HATR TRICKS **8 HAT TRICKS**

Hang on, *Ronaldo's* got eight hat tricks too!

CHAMPIONS LEAGUE HIGHLIGHTS

MAY 27, 2009

FINAL

Barcelona 2-0 Manchester United

*Messi's awesome headed goal helped secure the title—and the **TREBLE**—for Barcelona.*

APRIL 6, 2010

QUARTERFINAL SECOND LEG

Barcelona 4-1 Arsenal (6-3)

*Trailing 1-0 after 19 minutes, Messi hit back with one, two, three, **FOUR** goals. Amazing!*

MARCH 7, 2012

LAST-16 SECOND LEG

Barcelona 7-1 Bayer Leverkusen (10-2)

*Messi scored an incredible **FIVE** goals as Barca thrashed the German side.*

MAY 1, 2019

SEMIFINAL FIRST LEG

Barcelona 3-0 Liverpool

*Messi's stunning free kick was his second goal of the match—and his **600th** for Barcelona.*

HAT TRICK HERO

You already know that Messi has scored **four** and **five goals** in a single Champions League game. Here are some games where he only scored three.

Only three!

SEPTEMBER 18, 2013

GROUP STAGE

Barcelona 4-0 Ajax

*Messi's incredible **trio** of goals against Ajax included an awesome free kick.*

Ronaldo had scored a Champions League **hat trick** the day before this one.

OCTOBER 19, 2016

GROUP STAGE

Barcelona 4-0 Manchester City

*Pep Guardiola was now City's manager and Messi reminded his old boss how good he was with a **thrilling triple**.*

SEPTEMBER 18, 2018

GROUP STAGE

Barcelona 4-0 PSV Eindhoven

*Another Dutch team, another amazing free kick and another **hat-trick**. Messi's **48th** of his career.*

BAYERN BRACE

This was a tough fixture. **Messi, Suarez, Neymar,** and their teammates faced a strong Bayern side led by former Barca boss **Pep Guardiola.**

Boateng

It was **0–0** until the 77th minute, when Messi fired in a low, deadly shot. **1–0!**

Just three minutes later, Messi scored again. He turned past defender **Jerome Boateng,** who fell to the ground, and chipped the ball over the head of Bayern keeper **Manuel Neuer. 2–0!**

THAT'S GENIUS!

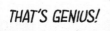

Neuer

Then **Neymar** made it **3–0** and Bayern were finished.

IT WAS ONE OF MESSI'S BEST PERFORMANCES.

After the game, the Barcelona manager **Luis Enrique** said:

"WITH MESSI, SOCCER IS EASIER. HE'S A PLAYER FROM ANOTHER DIMENSION. AND WE CAN ENJOY HIM EVERY DAY."

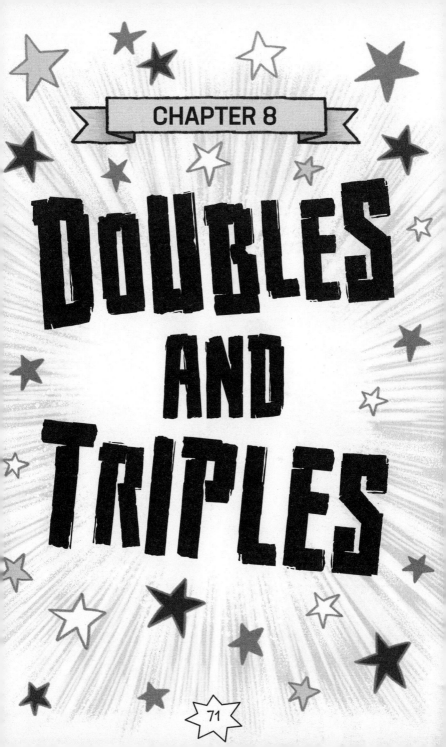

CHAPTER 8

DOUBLES AND TRIPLES

When Ronaldhino left Barcelona in 2008, Messi took the famous **number 10** shirt. **Messi** played with **Xavi** and **Iniesta** in midfield, and **Samuel Eto'o** and **Thierry Henry** up front.

The team played brilliantly together. One time, they beat Real Madrid **6-2** away from home.

IT WAS A *SPECIAL TEAM* FOR A *SPECIAL SEASON . . .*

TREBLE 2008-09

Barcelona beat **Athletic Bilbao 4–1** to win the **Copa del Rey**. . .

. . . finished **nine points** ahead of **Real Madrid** to win **La Liga** . . .

. . . and beat **Manchester United 2–0** to win the **Champions League.**

WHAM!

Messi scored **38 goals** that season.
Added to **Eto'o** and **Henry's** tally, it was

100 GOALS.

Barcelona and Messi had made **HISTORY.**
It was the **first time** that any Spanish
team had won a **TREBLE.**

They also won the **Supercopa de Espana,** the **UEFA Super Cup** and the **FIFA Club World Cup.**

THAT'S AN INCREDIBLE **SIX TROPHIES IN ONE YEAR.**

No other team has done that. *Ever!*

MY FIRST FOOTBALL FACTS

BALL

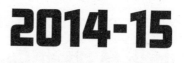

TREBLE 2014-15

Incredibly, **six** years later,

BARCELONA DID IT AGAIN!

It was Messi's **first season** playing with **Suarez** and **Neymar**.

THEY SCORED 122 GOALS!

They beat **Athletic Bilbao** again, this time **3–1**, to win the **Copa del Rey**.

Barcelona beatjust **two points** behind when they won **La Liga**.

The **Champions League** was sealed with a **3–1** win over **Juventus**.

They were the first team to win a *treble*, twice!

Is two **TREBLES** enough for Messi?
No way! He has also
helped Barcelona win
three **DOUBLES!**

2010–11
La Liga
Champions League

2015–16
La Liga
Copa del Rey

2017–18
La Liga
Copa del Rey

CHAPTER 9

ARGENTINE ICON

OLYMPIC MEDAL WINNER, BEIJING 2008

Messi teamed up with Zabaleta and Aguero again as part of Argentina's Olympic team for the **2008 Olympic Games** in Beijing. **Angel di Maria** was also in the side.

They beat **Brazil 3–0** in the semifinal and **Nigeria 1–0** in the final to win . . .

OLYMPIC GOLD.

Leo says that the Olympics was was one of the ***most beautiful memories of his career.***
WINNING GOLD
by Vic Tree

In **2016,** Messi retired from international soccer. But the whole country, **including the president,** asked him to come back.

SO HE DID!

And then in **2021,** Messi finally won a major international trophy as **Argentina beat Brazil** to win the **Copa America.**

MESSI'S ARGENTINA RECORD

CAPS	GOALS	ASSISTS
175	103	56

Messi is Argentina's **most capped** player.

WORLD CUP FINAL

ARGENTINA 3-3 FRANCE *(4-2 on penalties)*

LUSAIL STADIUM, QATAR

The holders France faced tournament favorites **Argentina** in what was billed as a showdown between **Mess**i and **Kylian Mbappe.** And what a match it was!

Argentina dominated for **80 minutes** with **Messi** and **Angel Di Maria** giving them a 2-0 lead. Then, in a breathtaking final 10 minutes, **Mbappe** scored from the spot and quickly equalized with an incredible volley to force extra time.

Messi stepped up to restore Argentina's lead, only for Mbappe's late penalty to take the game to the shootout, where the South Americans triumphed. **INCREDIBLE scenes!**

It was hailed as the

GREATEST WORLD CUP FINAL – EVER . . .

. . . and Messi had won soccer's **biggest prize!**

CHAPTER 10

LA LIGA LIFE

LA LIGA GOAL MACHINE

In 17 seasons, Messi scored an incredible **474 goals** for Barcelona in La Liga.

Nobody has **scored more** La Liga **goals** than **Messi.** **EVER.**

SEASON	APPEARANCES	GOALS
2004-05	7	1
2005-06	17	6
2006-07	26	14
2007-08	28	10
2008-09	31	23
2009-10	35	34
2010-11	33	31
2011-12	37	50
2012-13	32	46
2013-14	31	28
2014-15	38	43
2015-16	33	26
2016-17	34	37
2017-18	36	34
2018-19	34	36
2019-20	33	25
2020-21	35	30
TOTAL	520	474

MESSI'S RECORD IN LA LIGA IS

UNBELIEVABLE.

LA LIGA TOP SCORER

2009-10 **34** GOALS

2011-12 **50** GOALS

2012-13 **46** GOALS

2016-17 **37** GOALS

2017-18 **34** GOALS

2018-19 **36** GOALS

2019-20 **25** GOALS

2020-21 **30** GOALS

50 GOALS IN LA LIGA 2011-12

The **most goals ever scored** by a player **in one season** in La Liga.

36 LA LIGA HAT-TRICKS

A record for Barcelona.

20+ LA LIGA GOALS FOR
13 SEASONS IN A ROW

Messi is the ONLY player to do this.

MOST ASSISTS
IN LA LIGA
192

LA LIGA'S ALL-TIME
TOP SCORER
474

MOST ASSISTS IN A
SINGLE LA LIGA SEASON
21 (2019-20)

MOST FREE KICK GOALS
SCORED IN LA LIGA
39

MOST HAT-TRICKS SCORED
IN A LA LIGA SEASON
8

Has anyone else
done this?

Er, yes. **Ronaldo!**

RONALDO
RULES

HAT-TRICK HERO

Messi has scored an incredible **36 hat tricks** in **La Liga**. These are some of his best.

MARCH 10, 2007

Barcelona 3-3 Real Madrid

*Messi's first hat trick for Barcelona was against their great rivals Real Madrid. **Wow!***

FEBRUARY 19, 2012

Barcelona 5-1 Valencia

*Messi scored **FOUR** of five Barca goals. One of **FOUR** hat tricks for Messi against Valencia.*

DECEMBER 7, 2019

BARCELONA 5-2 MALLORCA

*This hat trick was Messi's **35th** in La Liga – breaking the record held by **Ronaldo** for **Real Madrid**.*

EL CLASICO CLASSICS

Barcelona versus **Real Madrid** is one of

the biggest games in world soccer. It's called

EL CLASICO.

MAY 2, 2009

Real Madrid 2-6 Barcelona

*Messi scored two and his old friend **Gerard Pique** got the sixth goal as Madrid were hammered at home.*

NOVEMBER 29, 2010

Barcelona 5-0 Real Madrid

*No goals from Messi, but two assists helped deliver this thumping. It was Madrid manager Jose Mourinho's first **El Clasico.***

MARCH 23, 2014

Real Madrid 3-4 Barcelona

*A **Ronaldo** penalty, Sergio Ramos sent off and Messi scored two penalties to complete his hat trick. **A thriller of a game!***

APRIL 23, 2017

Real Madrid 2-Barcelona 3

Messi's stoppage-time goal finished this end-of-season monster El Clasico. It was his **500th goal** *for Barcelona and he celebrated taking off his shirt and holding it up for the Barca fans.* **Nice.**

He got a yellow card for doing this!

CHAPTER 11

MESSI VS. RONALDO

The **argument** about **who's the best** will go on **forever.**

The Ballon d'Or (The Golden Ball)

is a **prize** awarded to

the **best soccer player**

each year.

LOOK AT THE RESULTS SINCE RONALDO WON IT FIRST.

YEAR	1ST PLACE	2ND PLACE
2008	RONALDO	MESSI
2009	MESSI	RONALDO
2010	MESSI	ANDRES INIESTA
2011	MESSI	RONALDO

HELLO!

YEAR	1ST PLACE	2ND PLACE
2012	MESSI	RONALDO
2013	RONALDO	MESSI
2014	RONALDO	MESSI
2015	MESSI	RONALDO
2016	RONALDO	MESSI
2017	RONALDO	MESSI
2018	LUKA MODRIC	RONALDO
2019	MESSI	VIRGIL VAN DIJK
2021	MESSI	ROBERT LEWANDOWSKI

GRRR!

The **2020** award was cancelled because of the **Covid-19 pandemic**

INTERNATIONAL PENALTIES SCORED
24 18

CHAMPIONS LEAGUE MEDALS
4 5

CHAMPIONS LEAGUE GOALS
129 141

WORLD CUP GOALS
13 8

LEAGUE TITLES
11 7

DOMESTIC CUP TITLES
7 6

GOLDEN SHOE WINS
6 4

MESSI vs RONALDO
in LA LIGA

SEASON	MESSI GOALS	RONALDO GOALS
2009-10	34	26
2010-11	31	40
2011-12	50	46
2012-13	46	34
2013-14	28	31
2014-15	43	48
2015-16	26	35
2016-17	37	25
2017-18	34	26
TOTAL	**329**	**311**

CHAPTER 12

SUPER MESSI

SUPER FLEA

Messi is one of the **fastest** players in the world—he's recorded a speed of

20.2 MPH!

He's not the fastest player, but nobody **dribbles the ball** at speed like Messi.

FANTASTIC FEINTS

The **BODY FEINT** is where a player tricks

his opponent into

thinking he's **going**

one way . . .

NUTMEG MASTER

The **NUTMEG** is a trick where a player moves

the ball between his opponent's legs.

Nigel Nutmeg, an actual nutmeg!

NUTMEGS RULE!

112

Messi is **superb** at nutmegs. Sometimes he passes to a teammate, but when Messi picks the ball up again and continues his run, it's **extra-special.**

SOMETIMES, A MESSI NUTMEG FLOORS THE OPPOSITION PLAYER!

"WHAT LEO DOES IS SO INCREDIBLE THAT I HAVE TO BE CAREFUL NOT TO STAND STILL WATCHING HIM MAKE HIS MOVES."

Thierry Henry, Messi's teammate at Barcelona - 2007-10

114

CHAPTER 13

THE G.O.A.T?

(GREATEST OF ALL TIME)

In the summer of **2021**, every Barcelona fan's **nightmare** became a **reality.** Messi **LEFT** to join **Paris Saint-Germain.**

GOODBYE AND THANK YOU!

It was a new adventure, but with his old friend **NEYMAR** and the French super striker **KYLIAN MBAPPE.**

MBAPPE

NEYMAR

Messi ended the year with another win as he picked up the **Ballon d'Or** for a record-breaking **SEVENTH** time.

After **two seasons** at PSG, Messi moved to the **USA** in 2023, signing for **David Beckham's** MLS club Inter Miami.

The Argentinian made a **dream debut**, scoring a game-winning **free-kick** in the **94th minute** and showing the **crowd** the magic he brings to American league.

POW!

119

MESSI RECORDS
(YOU MIGHT NOT KNOW)

MOST GOALS SCORED IN A CALENDAR YEAR: **91** (2012)

MOST ASSISTS IN THE COPA AMERICA: **17**

YOUNGEST PLAYER TO SCORE **400+** GOALS FOR A SINGLE EUROPEAN CLUB

MOST GOALS SCORED IN LA LIGA EL CLÁSICO MATCHES: **26**

MOST INTERNATIONAL GOALS BY A SOUTH AMERICAN MALE PLAYER: **98**

ONLY PLAYER TO SCORE **60+** GOALS IN BACK-TO-BACK SEASONS: 2011-12 **(73)** AND 2012-13 **(60)**.

YOUNGEST PLAYER TO REACH **100** CHAMPIONS LEAGUE APPEARANCES.

MOST BRACES (TWO GOALS) IN LA LIGA: **116**

MOST FREE KICKS SCORED FOR BARCELONA: **50**

LEGENDS

Messi will go down in history as one of the **giants of soccer.**

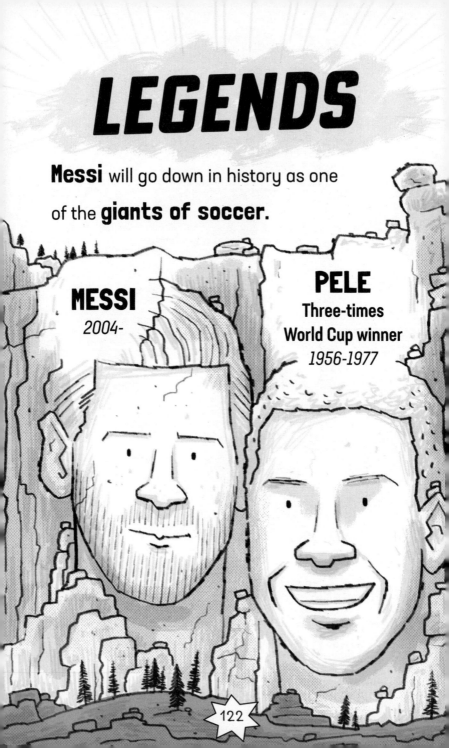

MESSI
2004-

PELE
Three-times
World Cup winner
1956-1977

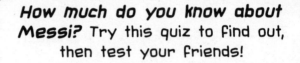

QUIZ TIME!

How much do you know about **Messi?** Try this quiz to find out, then test your friends!

1. How many times has Messi won La Liga?

----

2. Which team did he play for before Barcelona?

----

3. Name the two other players in 'MSN'?

----

4. Who called Leo his 'Little Brother'?

----

5. In which year did he win his first Ballon d'Or?

----

6. In which year did Messi win an Olympic Gold Medal?

----

7. How many goals did he score in La Liga in 2011-12?

----

8. Who is Messi's biggest rival in soccer?

----

9. Which team did Messi join in 2021?

----

10. How many goals did Messi score in the 2022 World Cup?

The answers are on the next page. *But no peeking!*

ANSWERS

1. 10
2. Newell's Old Boys
3. Luis Suarez, Neymar
4. Ronaldinho
5. 2009
6. 2008
7. 50
8. Cristiano Ronaldo
9. Paris Saint-Germain
10. Seven

MESSI:
WORDS YOU NEED TO KNOW

Ballon d'Or
Award given to the male player who has played the best over a year. Awarded each December by *France Football* magazine.

Copa Del Rey
Spanish knockout cup competition.

FIFA Club World Cup
Knockout cup competition between clubs from around the world.

La Liga
The top soccer league in Spain.

El Clasico
The match between Barcelona and Real Madrid.

UEFA Champions League
European club competition held every year. The winner is the best team in Europe.

Supercopa de Espana
Match played between the La Liga champions and the winners of the Copa Del Rey.

ABOUT THE AUTHORS

Simon's first job was at the Science Museum, making paper aeroplanes, and blowing bubbles big enough for your dad to stand in. Since then he's written all sorts of books about the stuff he likes, from dinosaurs and rockets, to llamas, loud music and of course, soccer. Simon has supported English club Ipswich Town since they won the FA Cup in 1978 (it's true - look it up) and once sat next to Rio Ferdinand on a train. He lives in Kent, UK, with his wife and daughter, a dog and a cat.

Dan has drawn silly pictures since he could hold a crayon. Then he grew up and started making books about stuff like trucks, space, people's jobs, *Doctor Who,* and *Star Wars.* Dan remembers Ipswich Town winning the FA Cup but he didn't watch it because he was too busy making a Viking ship out of brown paper. As a result, he knows more about Vikings than soccer. Dan lives in Suffolk, UK, with his wife, son, daughter, and a dog that takes him for very long walks.